Christina Applegate: From Comedy to Courage

A Life Lived in Laughter and Bravery

Alice C. Austin

Table Of Contents

INTRODUCTION

Christina Applegate has a distinct position in the pantheon of charming stars in Hollywood. Her story, which is characterised by an infectious laugh and an unbreakable spirit, is proof of the transformational potential of bravery and resiliency. More than just a biography, "Christina Applegate: From Comedy to Courage - A Life Lived in Laughter and Bravery" is a story that entwines the strands of a public life lived in the spotlight with the inner struggles waged behind closed doors.

Christina was born into a family with strong ties to the entertainment business and her narrative began under the glittering lights of Hollywood. It seemed almost inevitable that she would end up on stage and film. However, the unwritten aspect of her career was the unwavering determination she would display. Christina's life has been an emotional rollercoaster filled with highs and lows, joy and sorrow, starting with her breakthrough role as the stereotypical adolescent in "Married... with Children" and continuing with her brave fight with breast cancer.

This book explores how Christina's early years in front of the camera formed her as an actor and as a person, going deep into the core of her humorous brilliance. It honours her successes in the movies and her surprising turns on Broadway, demonstrating her adaptability and love for what she does. It doesn't, however, skirt over the most difficult parts, when her strength really came through. Her battle with cancer was more than simply a personal one; she utilised her position to raise awareness and provide support for those going through similar struggles, turning her illness into a source of inspiration for many.

"A Life Lived in Laughter and Bravery" is a patchwork of events that characterise Christina Applegate's legacy as a person and an actor. It is a tale of how one woman's bravery can inspire a generation, how laughter can be a source of strength, and how celebrity can be used for the greater good. Turn the pages to meet Christina

Christina Applegate

Applegate, the person you recognize from the screen and the one you don't, a woman who has smiled her way through adversity and come out stronger than before.

CHAPTER 1: ROOTS OF COMEDY

Early Life In Hollywood

In Hollywood, California, on November 25, 1971, Christina Applegate was born. When she was a newborn, actress Nancy Priddy and record producer Bob Applegate were divorced. Her mother, who had fame as an actress in her own right and made appearances in a number of TV series and motion pictures in the 1960s and 1970s, reared Christina.

Being up in the centre of Hollywood, Christina was first introduced to the entertainment business at a very early age. At the age of three months, she starred in her first advertisement, playing a baby bottle for Playtex. Christina had already secured her first television appearance at the age of three, appearing as a guest star on the sitcom "Days of our Lives."

Christina developed her innate acting ability as a young age by continuing to obtain different TV and commercial jobs. The year 1987 saw her breakthrough role when she was chosen to play the glamorous but endearing Kelly Bundy in the popular Fox comedy "Married... with Children." Christina rose to fame at the age of 15, and the program went on to become a cultural phenomenon in the late 1980s and early 1990s.

Throughout her tenure on "Married... with Children," Christina made a concerted effort to manage her developing acting career with a somewhat typical adolescent life. Despite juggling a hectic filming schedule, she attended a nearby high school in the San Fernando Valley. Christina used to spend a lot of time with her co-stars in between shoots, becoming good friends with actors like Ed O'Neill and Katey Sagal, who portrayed her parents on TV.

Even when "Married... with Children" became popular, Christina was certain that she wouldn't be limited to the simple, blonde role that she played. She was always searching for ways to show off her range as an actor. Her serious parts started to emerge in the early 1990s, when she made appearances in TV movies and cameos on shows like "The Trials of Rosie O'Neill" and "21 Jump Street."

Christina took advantage of the opportunity to go into feature picture work when "Married... with Children" was coming to a close in the mid-1990s. Along with more sombre dramas like "The Big Hit" and "Wonderland," she also found parts in comedies like "Mars Attacks!" and "Anchorman: The Legend of Ron Burgundy."

Christina never gave in to the temptations that have befallen so many budding Hollywood stars; instead, she stayed sensible and committed throughout her early career. She gave thanks to both her mother's direction and her own diligent work ethic for keeping her on the correct path. Christina was determined to have a long-lasting, diverse career in the entertainment business, and her early years in Hollywood set the groundwork for that.

Family Influence

Christina Applegate, an actress's daughter raised in the centre of Hollywood, was surrounded by the entertainment business from an early age. However, her early life and developing profession were most significantly influenced by her family, both her familial and extended relatives.

In the 1960s and 1970s, Nancy Priddy, Christina's mother, worked as an actress and had several appearances in movies and television series. Nancy, who raised Christina alone, instilled in her a strong respect and work ethic for the performing arts. Christina went to auditions with her mother from a young age, often seeing her practice and act. Christina's interest in and ambition to pursue acting as a profession were spurred by her first-hand experience with the process.

Despite the fact that Christina's actual father was Bob Applegate, a record producer, her growth was greatly influenced by her stepfather, musician and producer Russ Kunkel. Christina looked up to Kunkel, who had married Nancy while she was only a child, and he served as a mentor and father figure to her. He supported her developing acting ambitions and exposed her to music, all while fostering her creative interests.

Kunkel's early contacts in the entertainment world also provided Christina with opportunities. She was able to get her first acting roles via his networks, including her baby debut in a Playtex ad. Later on, Kunkel guided Christina through the financial side of Hollywood, helping her with contract negotiations and career management.

Christina received encouragement and motivation from her extended family members who were also in the entertainment industry, in addition to her close relatives. Actress Lee Grinner Gladney, her grandmother, starred in beloved movies including "Bonnie and Clyde." Additionally, her great-uncle, Richard Cromwell, was an actor who appeared in several Hollywood films during the Golden Age.

Christina was raised with a profound awareness and enthusiasm for the entertainment industry because of her family's long history in show business. She saw the highs and lows, as well as the demands and difficulties, of juggling a career in performing. She had a maturity and insight that many young performers lacked because of her insider's viewpoint.

Christina's family gave her a solid, grounded base that helped her stay focused throughout the chaotic early stages of her career. Thanks in large part to her loved ones' support and direction, Christina managed to stay focused and level-headed while other young stars fell victim to the traps of Hollywood.

Christina's family stood at her side every step of the way as her career took off thanks to the enormous popularity of "Married... with Children" in the late 80s and early 90s. They provided her with a secure, caring atmosphere away from the limelight, allowing her to grow and flourish as a person and an actor.

Christina's background and family ties gave her a natural grasp of the entertainment world, which helped her immensely in her early career. Christina was well positioned for long-term success in Hollywood because of this solid foundation, which was built on the knowledge and experiences of those who came before her.

Beginnings In Acting

Christina Applegate was destined for a career in theatre and film from the day of her birth. Being the daughter of a record producer and an actress, Christina was raised in the entertainment business.

Christina starred in her first acting role in a Playtex baby bottle ad at the age of three months. A career of performing was paved with this early camera experience.

Casting directors saw Christina's innate skill and personality as she matured into a toddler. She appeared as a guest star in her first television appearance at the early age of three, in an episode of the serial opera "Days of our

Lives." Even though it was a small role, Christina experienced the bright lights and lively energy of a TV set for the first time.

Christina kept booking acting roles throughout her youth, always with the encouragement of her mother Nancy Priddy, who was also in the business. Christina embraced every chance she had, whether it was a voice-over, a minor TV guest part, or a commercial, with a professionalism and excitement that belied her youthful age.

Christina's breakthrough performance occurred in 1987 when, at the tender age of 15, she was chosen to play the adored ditz Kelly Bundy in the popular Fox comedy "Married... with Children." In the end, this role would define her early career and launch her into the spotlight.

It was not a simple task to play Kelly. Dozens of other young actresses fiercely competed with Christina for the coveted part. However, the show's creators were won over by her ability to flawlessly embody the character's mix of ditzy charm and underlying intellect. Christina immediately won over the crew and actors with her improvisational abilities and great comic timing during the first table read.

Christina's celebrity soared when "Married... with Children" became a cultural phenomenon in the late 1980s and early 1990s. Kelly Bundy's huge hair, short skirts, and Valley Girl demeanour made her an immediately recognized stereotype, and she soon became well-known.

Christina, however, never wavered from her love of acting, even as she revelled in the show's popularity. She developed her craft on the "Married... with Children" stage, playing with both physical and sentimental humour. Additionally, she would often watch the seasoned performers on stage in between takes, picking up their tips and tricks.

Outside of her work on the sitcom, Christina looked for chances to demonstrate her flexibility. She demonstrated that she was more than a one-trick pony by accepting guest parts in serious television shows including "The Trials of Rosie O'Neill" and "21 Jump Street." Her will to not be limited to the stereotype of a simple-minded blonde heroine set the stage for a long and diversified career.

Christina never let the perks of celebrity get to her, and she always maintained an amazing level of concentration and groundedness. She acknowledged that she stayed on the correct path because of her mother's advice and her own diligent work ethic. Christina stayed dedicated to her profession even as a teenager at the height of her comedy fame, setting the stage for an extraordinary career spanning decades.

CHAPTER 2: RISING STAR

Breakthrough Roles

It wasn't an easy path to the A-list for Christina Applegate to become a Hollywood celebrity. It all started with laughter galore on a program that dared to be outrageous, a dash of blonde ambition, and a pinch of youthful disobedience.

Kelly Bundy enters the picture. Christina was fifteen when she got the part that would lead to her big break: the famous, naive, and hilariously funny Kelly on Fox's comedy "Married... with Children." The program, which centred on the dysfunctional Bundy family and was a biting social satire, was risky. However, it paid off handsomely, turning into a craze in pop culture and launching Applegate and other young stars into the public eye.

Kelly Bundy embodied the stereotypical "dumb blonde," with her tight miniskirts, bleach-blonde hair, and a vocabulary that seldom went past "Duh" and "Whoa." But Christina gave Kelly an unexpected tenderness and sensitivity underneath the vacuous surface. She was the perfect antithesis of her obnoxious sister, the perennially grouchy Al Bundy, and his continually irritated wife, Peggy. For an astounding eleven seasons, viewers were captivated by the dysfunctional family dynamic they jointly crafted.

Delivering punchlines wasn't the only thing required to play Kelly. Christina played the part with a physicality and comic timing that were surprising for someone so young. She was an expert at the timed-exasperated sigh, the slow burn, and the eye roll. Kelly's infamous chuckle became as well-known as her eccentric attire. Although some would laugh at the complexity of the part, Christina's comic gift was what made Kelly Bundy so hilarious.

"Married... with Children" served as Christina's trial run. She had more than simply a charming appearance; she was a formidable comic. She was able to display her unquestionable star power, her ability to connect with an audience, and her comic skills on the program. Her opportunities to pursue parts outside of sitcoms were expanded as a result.

However, Kelly Bundy had two sides. It took some time for viewers to perceive Christina in a new light since the character's success came to be associated with the movie. But Christina wasn't going to let the "dumb blonde" stereotype define her. She proactively sought out parts that tested her and allowed her to show off her versatility as an actor.

This diligence was fruitful. Christina took up a number of varied jobs once the season of "Married... with Children" concluded. She voiced characters in animated flicks, acted in romantic comedies such as "The Sweetest Thing," and even took on tragic parts in movies like "Notes on a Scandal."

However, she continued to be drawn to television. She portrayed Samantha Who? in 2007, a lady attempting to reconstruct her life after suffering from amnesia. The program won praise from critics and cemented Christina's reputation as a gifted comedy performer.

Christina had a standout performance in the Netflix dark comedy "Dead to Me" more recently. Christina demonstrated her dramatic depth and emotional nuance when she portrayed Jen, a heartbroken widow who develops an odd friendship with another lady (played by Linda Cardellini). She gained critical acclaim and a new following as a result of the performance.

The transformation of Christina Applegate from teenage movie star to well-known actress is evidence of her brilliance, tenacity, and daring spirit. Though Christina's career has flourished well beyond that legendary role, Kelly Bundy will always be a part of her reputation. She has shown her ability to be a talented performer by making you laugh till you weep and leaving you wanting more.

Successes In Comedy

Christina Applegate showcased her innate comic abilities from the time she first appeared on television as the endearingly simple-minded Kelly Bundy in the popular comedy "Married... with Children." She became an overnight sensation because of her uncanny ability to combine physical comedy, timing, and likeability.

Christina's portrayal as the sultry blonde daughter in "Married... with Children" solidified her reputation as a comic masterwork during the late 80s and early 90s as the show became a pop cultural success. She captured Kelly's corny mannerisms and malapropisms flawlessly, leaving audiences in stitches week after week. Her relationship with co-stars Ed O'Neill and Katey Sagal produced a lovable family dynamic that drew viewers in.

Christina's ability to give the one-note Kelly surprising depth and nuance was what made her comic performance on the program so amazing. Christina managed to bring empathy and sensitivity to the role, despite the fact that the character was often the target of jokes. The wide-ranging hilarity was counterbalanced by poignant and sincere moments.

After her breakthrough performance on "Married... with Children," Christina looked for other chances to demonstrate her humorous abilities. She showed herself to be a very flexible performer, equally adept at verbal wit, physical comedy, and more subdued humour.

Christina started her shift into feature picture work in the mid-1990s, when "Married... with Children" was coming to an end. Her career took her to prominent comedic parts in films such as Tim Burton's "Mars Attacks!" and Will Ferrell's "Anchorman: The Legend of Ron Burgundy." She showed off her acute improvisational skills and talent for enhancing the content with her flawless timing and delivery in each.

Christina's triumph in the movies further strengthened her position as a major force in comedy. She was a great addition to the business because of her amazing ability to portray characters who were both wide and exaggerated and those that were more realistic and sympathetic. Producers and directors were aware of her ability to extract humour from even the most ordinary circumstances.

As Christina's career developed, she kept looking for lucrative and demanding comedic roles that stretched the limits of her abilities. She embraced riskier, more subversive material, not hesitant to push the boundaries with her performances or take on contentious subjects.

One of the most notable aspects of Christina's subsequent comedy career was her lead part in the critically praised sitcom "Up All Night" during the early 2010s. Christina had an amazing talent for both physical humour and subtle emotional storytelling in her role as Reagan, a successful executive juggling the pressures of her work with the challenges of being a new mother.

Christina has received praise for her comic skills from both audiences and reviewers throughout the course of her multi-decade career. One of the most gifted and adaptable comic actors of her time, she is renowned for her ability to switch between slapstick humour and nuanced wit with ease.

Three things have contributed to Christina's success in the comedy industry: her natural talent, her unwavering work ethic, and her daring willingness to take chances. She has consistently pushed the bounds of what is considered appropriate for a "funny" actress, leaving an enduring and distinctive mark on the entertainment industry.

Challenges And Setbacks

Red carpet appearances and award show victories weren't Christina Applegate's only stops during her Hollywood journey. Beneath her vivacious grin and witty repartee, there were a sequence of obstacles that tried her fortitude and redefined her power.

"Married... with Children" cast a long shadow. Kelly Bundy undoubtedly started her career, but it also had unintended consequences. She was often stereotyped as the traditional stupid blonde by both critics and viewers. Getting parts outside of sitcoms proved to be challenging.

Despite her several auditions, she was never cast in favour of women without the "Kelly Bundy baggage."

It hurts to be rejected like this. Christina understood she was much more than just a funny one-liner. She yearned for chances to show off her dramatic range and delve deeper into personalities. One of the things that frustrated her the most was trying to be taken seriously as an actor.

Then the health worries started. Christina was 36 years old in 2008 when she received her breast cancer diagnosis. The news came as a terrible shock. She was obliged to put her health above her work and take a step back after undergoing a double mastectomy and exhausting chemotherapy treatments. Despite the extreme mental and physical stress of the time, Christina faced it with her usual bravery and tenacity.

Christina's health challenges would not end with cancer. She disclosed her multiple sclerosis (MS) diagnosis in 2021, years after being diagnosed. MS is a chronic neurological disorder that affects the central nervous system. She was set to start shooting the third season of "Dead to Me" when she received the diagnosis. Her acting career and the show's future were both tainted by uncertainty.

The "Dead to Me" filming with MS turned out to be a huge difficulty. Her illness resulted in numbness, exhaustion, and issues with balance. Some days it seemed like a success just to get through a scene. Christina pushed herself to the edge, determined not to let MS control her career, and the staff worked nonstop to meet her requirements.

Christina found great strength in the public support that she received after her MS diagnosis. Many others who are fighting chronic ailments found resonance in her narrative. She unintentionally turned into a spokesperson for MS awareness and the value of maintaining optimism in the face of hardship.

Christina Applegate is an example of someone who perseveres in the face of adversity. She overcame major health obstacles and type casting to come out stronger on the other side. Her story serves as an inspiration, showing that

Christina Applegate

despite life's most difficult blows, one can always find the will to persevere and the ability to reinvent oneself.

CHAPTER 3: PERSONAL STRUGGLES

Health Battles

The tale of Christina Applegate goes much beyond the amusements seen on TV. Her path has been dotted by major health setbacks that required extraordinary fortitude and tenacity.

2008 was the first significant setback. Christina was 36 years old when she received her breast cancer diagnosis. The shock of this unexpected revelation rocked her world. Not only was the diagnosis a personal setback, but it also required her to pause her profession in order to concentrate on her care.

Christina had a double mastectomy, which involves the removal of both breasts. Chemotherapy, an arduous treatment that employs powerful medications to eradicate cancer cells, came next. There was a severe mental and bodily toll. She struggled with the anxiety and uncertainty of the illness in addition to experiencing exhaustion, nausea, and hair loss.

Christina showed amazing bravery throughout this situation. She never held back while telling her tale to spread the word about breast cancer and how crucial early diagnosis is. She became an inspiration to other ladies who were going through similar struggles.

Christina, who had fought illness and had a successful course of treatment, seemed to be eager to resume her acting career. However, life had other ideas. While shooting the third season of her popular Netflix series "Dead to Me," Christina was diagnosed with multiple sclerosis (MS) in 2021, which led to yet another life-altering diagnosis.

Multiple Sclerosis is a long-term neurological disorder affecting the central nervous system. It interferes with the information transfer between the brain and the body, leading to a range of symptoms such as exhaustion, numbness, weakened muscles, blurred vision, and imbalance difficulties.

It was a dreadful diagnosis. It not only put her general health in jeopardy but also clouded her acting career. The physical demands of the part looked unachievable just before "Dead to Me" filming started.

Christina, nevertheless, never backs down from a task. She was adamant about finishing the play she loved. It became an uphill fight to film. It was challenging to endure lengthy days on set due to the weariness brought on by multiple sclerosis. Her movement and coordination were impacted by the numbness and balance issues.

The cast of "Dead to Me" came through big time, putting forth endless effort to make Christina feel comfortable and supported. To reduce hazards, they changed the filming schedules, added extra breaks, and put safety precautions in place.

Christina then went to the edge of her own comfort zone. She refused to allow MS to define or direct her professional path. She certainly had days when she was frustrated and tired, but her perseverance and unflinching spirit got the better of her.

Many people connected with Christina's determination to be transparent about her MS diagnosis. It gave people with chronic diseases hope and support. She became an advocate for spreading knowledge about multiple sclerosis and the value of maintaining optimism in the face of hardship.

Christina Applegate's health struggles are evidence of her resolute fortitude and spirit of defiance. She has bravely and gracefully battled MS and cancer, coming out stronger and more motivated than before. Her experience serves as motivation and a reminder that despite life's most difficult blows, one has the willpower to persevere and the fortitude to get through.

Finding Strength Through Adversity

Christina Applegate's journey to fame hasn't always been straightforward. She has encountered enormous emotional and professional obstacles at different stages in her remarkable career that would have crushed many performers. Christina, however, has shown unflinching tenacity and drive throughout, becoming stronger and more determined to succeed despite every setback.

During the height of her breakthrough success on the popular comedy "Married... with Children" in the late 1980s, Christina faced one of the first trials of her resilience. Christina had difficulties dealing with the demands of entering the Hollywood limelight at such a young age, even in spite of the show's enormous success and her standing as a budding young star. She suffered from low self-esteem and body image as a result of the media's unceasing focus and severe scrutiny.

Christina, nevertheless, deliberately chose to take charge of her story rather than allowing these fears to rule her. She emerged as a vocal supporter of body acceptance and used her position to criticise the unattainable beauty standards in Hollywood. Christina was emboldened by her stubborn attitude, and it also served as an inspiration to many young women who could relate to her personal hardships.

Christina would have to withstand an even bigger challenge years later when, at the age of 36, she was given a breast cancer diagnosis in 2008. She was enjoying a significant career comeback with high-profile parts in critically praised drama "Samantha Who?" and popular flicks "Anchorman" when the tragic news broke. Christina, however, faced her battle with the illness with the same unflinching will that had shaped her career and refused to let the news derail her.

Christina stayed strong throughout her treatment, finding comfort in her family's and close friends' love and support. She had reconstructive surgery and a double mastectomy, but she didn't allow the experience to make her less of a person or her love of performing. Christina also used her experience to advocate for research and awareness of breast cancer when she was declared cancer-free.

Christina has had hardships outside of her personal life as well. She has overcome many obstacles and disappointments in her career over the years, including unsuccessful TV pilots and poorly received movies. She has, however, persevered unwaveringly, seeing every setback as a chance to improve and refine her skills.

Christina's ability to strike a balance between her unrelenting resolve and a feeling of humility and honesty is maybe what makes her strength most impressive. She has never been afraid to face up to her flaws and weaknesses and has always used them to build stronger connections with her audiences. Her appeal as a performer and public figure has only increased as a result of her openness to be vulnerable and transparent.

Christina has continuously shown throughout her career that her real strength is not in her achievements or honours but rather in her capacity to face challenges head-on with poise, resiliency, and an unwavering sense of self. She has emerged as a global inspiration for women and aspiring performers, proving that real power comes from having the guts to take on and conquer even the most difficult obstacles rather than from being flawless.

Christina's unrelenting passion and tenacity will definitely continue to be her guiding lights as she navigates the always shifting Hollywood scene. She has often shown that she has the courage and strength to overcome any hardship and come out stronger than before.

CHAPTER 4: COMEDY QUEEN

Iconic Roles

Christina Applegate has played a variety of noteworthy and critically praised parts throughout her two decades in the entertainment business, solidifying her place as one of the most gifted and adaptable actors of her time. Christina has continuously shown her ability to enthral viewers with her depth and variety, from her breakthrough role as the sultry Kelly Bundy on the popular comedy "Married... with Children" to her subtle serious work in more recent years.

Without a doubt, Christina's first rise to fame came from her performance as Kelly Bundy on "Married... with Children." She made her stage debut in 1987 at the early age of 15, and she captured the essence of the character's ideal combination of airheaded charm and underlying intellect with ease. Christina's physical comedy skills and great comic timing had fans in stitches week after week. Christina's portrayal of Kelly Bundy laid the groundwork for the character's iconic status in pop culture.

Christina, nevertheless, was resolved not to fit the stereotype of a simple-minded blonde. During the eleven-season span of the program, she never stopped looking for chances to demonstrate her depth and range as an actor. Christina would inject Kelly with unexpected emotional fragility in between the boisterous, comedic times, teasing the more subtle talents that lingered under the surface.

In the mid-1990s, when "Married... with Children" was about to end, Christina took advantage of the chance to go into feature picture work. She portrayed Susie, the naive yet kind-hearted daughter of Tom Jones, in Tim Burton's science fiction comedy "Mars Attacks!" in 1996, which became one of her most famous big-screen performances. Christina gave Susie a charming likeability that helped her transcend the film's overarching satire, by drawing on the same glitzy, effervescent qualities that had made Kelly Bundy so adored.

A few years later, Christina once again proved her comic skills with an exceptional role in the 2004 blockbuster "Anchorman: The Legend of Ron Burgundy." She held her own against the male-dominated cast in the movie as the aspirational and sassy Veronica Corningstone, more than holding her own with her precise timing and scathing wit. Christina was able to show off a new aspect of her comic range in the part, giving up the ditzy naivete of previous roles in favour of a more confident, aggressive presence.

Christina started taking on increasingly dramatic, complex parts as her career developed, which helped people recognize her abilities even more. One of Christina's greatest moments was when she landed the lead role in the Showtime series "Samantha Who?" in 2007. Christina received praise from critics for her nuanced depiction of an amnesic lady. Her portrayal of the character was highly praised due to her ability to skillfully blend authentic emotional depth with humorous sensibility.

Christina is a master of both physical and emotional humour; her work on the sitcom "Up All Night" in the early 2010s was the most recent example of this. She managed the difficulties of striking a balance between the demands of a hard job and the reality of a new mom as the powerful executive Reagan. Christina received high appreciation from both reviewers and fans for her masterful presentation of rich, genuine comedy.

Christina Applegate has amazed and delighted audiences with her wide range of abilities throughout her successful career. She has consistently shown that she is one of the most iconic and varied actors of her age, whether it be via the subtle emotional work of "Samantha Who? " or the comedic antics of "Married... with Children." Her standing as a genuine stage and cinema great has been cemented with each unforgettable part that has brought a new dimension to her impressive body of work.

Comedy Legacy

Christina Applegate has established herself as one of the most talented and significant comedy actors of her age during the course of her multi-decade career. Christina has continuously shown an almost unmatched grasp of the comedy art, from her breakthrough role as the sultry Kelly Bundy on the popular sitcom "Married... with Children" to her more recent lauded work in cinema and television.

Christina's legendary depiction of Kelly Bundy throughout the late 1980s and early 1990s was the primary factor in her first rise to fame and the establishment of her long-lasting comedic reputation. She delivered raucous laughter with her perfect timing and physical comedic talents, expertly capturing the character's combination of Valley Girl vapidity and unexpected depth week after week. Christina's performance became deeply embedded in the public psyche, and Kelly

Bundy became an immediately identifiable pop culture persona.

However, Christina's comic abilities went much beyond that one part. She has shown throughout her career that she is an extraordinarily flexible and adaptive performer, switching from broad slapstick and more subtle, character-driven comedy with ease. Christina always improved the material with her keen wit and natural comic instincts, whether she was portrayed as the sardonic Veronica Corningstone in "Anchorman" or the dim-witted Susie in "Mars Attacks!"

Christina's unabashed desire to take chances and push limits is one of the defining characteristics of her comedic career. She's never shied away from more daring, provocative stuff; she's not scared to take on contentious issues or subvert the expectations of her audience. She has gained critical recognition and a horde of loyal admirers because of her audacious and unabashed attitude to questioning the current status quo.

However, Christina's contribution to humour goes beyond her achievements in the spotlight. She has also advocated for more inclusion and portrayal of women and body acceptance in the entertainment business throughout her career by using her platform. In addition to giving many young artists more confidence, her vocal position on these matters has changed public perceptions of and expectations for comic women.

Christina's comic talent has been seen in more recent years in shows including the critically praised Showtime series "Samantha Who?" and the comedy "Up All Night." She established herself as a master of the art in these roles by showcasing her extraordinary ability to combine physical comedy with more grounded, emotionally impactful narrative.

Christina Applegate has had a lasting impression on the comedy industry in a variety of media, including television, movies, and even activism. Her contemporaries and hordes of admirers love and admire her for her adaptability, daring attitude, and unrelenting dedication to her work. And Christina's reputation will undoubtedly only continue to expand in prominence and importance as she pushes the envelope of what is conceivable for a comedy actor.

Christina Applegate, one of the most adored and esteemed comic performers in the entertainment business, made her debut as the legendary Kelly Bundy decades ago. She is now recognized as a genuine comedy icon, an inspiration to young actors of all origins and identities because of her unmatched body of work and unwavering commitment to advancing the genre.

CHAPTER 5: TRANSITION AND EVOLUTION

Dramatic Roles

Christina Applegate is well-known due to her hilarious timing and contagious laugh. But a passion for dramatic discovery blazed under the surface. It became a particular ambition for her to break out from the stereotype of the "dumb blonde" that she had formed with Kelly Bundy in "Married... with Children," and her path towards dramatic parts is a fascinating tale in and of itself.

The first moves were hesitant. Romantic comedies such as "The Sweetest Thing" used her charming comic style and alluded to a more profound emotional spectrum. The thrillers followed. "Don't Tell Mom the Babysitter's Dead" gave us a peek of her capacity to work through a frightening story. "Notes on a Scandal" marked a dramatic shift. Here,

Christina portrayed a cunning instructor next to Judi Dencht's dejected politician. A complex performance was required for the movie, since there were many competing emotions seething under the surface. Christina succeeded, winning praise from critics for portraying a woman that was both cunning and vulnerable.

This important acknowledgment created opportunities. In "Samantha Who?", a dramedy about a lady with amnesia putting together her life, she was cast in the starring role. She was able to delve into issues of self-discovery, grief, and identity via the program. Christina's skill at balancing sadness and comedy struck a chord with viewers.

However, "Dead to Me" marked Christina's true ascent to the dramatic forefront. In this role, she portrayed Jen, a bereaved widow who develops an unusual friendship with Linda Cardellini's character. The show delved deeply into the difficult subjects of forgiveness, remorse, and bereavement. Even Christina's most devoted followers were taken aback by her powerful performance, which displayed a real vulnerability and emotional depth. Through the series, she received critical acclaim as well as admiration from a whole new audience who regarded her as a genuinely talented serious actor rather than simply the humorous girl from comedies.

Christina's path to dramatic parts wasn't always easy to follow. Some questioned if Kelly Bundy was the pivotal moment in her career. Christina persisted anyway, unwaveringly passionate about showcasing her whole range. She deliberately pursued challenging parts that required emotional transparency and openness from her. She reinvented herself as an actor and defied expectations at the same time.

Christina Applegate is a living example of the strength of tenacity and creative development. She has shown that dramatic depth and comic genius can coexist, and that laughing and crying are two sides of the same coin. Her experience serves as a reminder to all performers that genuine talent is still hidden behind typecasting and is only waiting to be realised.

Versatility In Acting

Christina Applegate has shown again and again throughout the course of her distinguished career that she is among the most talented and nuanced actresses of her age. Christina has shown an unmatched versatility that few of her peers can match, showcasing everything from the broad, physical comedy of her breakout role on "Married... with Children" to the more nuanced, dramatic performances that have earned her critical acclaim in recent years.

Christina originally gained notoriety and became recognized as a master of comic timing and physical comedy during her star-making role as the sultry Kelly Bundy on the popular sitcom "Married... with Children" in the 1990s. She captured audiences' attention every week with her accurate depiction of the stereotypical Valley Girl, evoking wild laughter with her exaggerated demeanour and keen humour.

However, Christina was able to give Kelly depth and subtlety even within the parameters of that apparently one-note character, hinting at the more nuanced emotional range that was hidden under the surface. She created a multifaceted portrayal that went against expectations by skillfully striking a balance between the character's naive pranks and real vulnerability.

While "Married... with Children" developed, Christina kept looking for chances to show off her flexibility. She demonstrated that she was more than just a comedy actor by accepting guest roles in more serious television shows like "21 Jump Street" and "The Trials of Rosie O'Neill." Audiences and reviewers alike were amazed by her natural aptitude and versatility as she moved between comedy and drama with ease.

Christina finally got the opportunity to showcase her flexibility on the big screen when the cherished sitcom ended in the mid-1990s. She has played a variety of parts throughout the following decades, ranging from broad humour in "Mars Attacks!" to sharper, more subversive wit in "Anchorman: The Legend of Ron Burgundy."

Christina started to go into more serious and subtle areas even as she solidified her reputation as a comedy expert. One of Christina's most memorable roles was her highly praised appearance in the late 2000s Showtime series "Samantha Who?" Christina played an emotionally complex and multi-layered amnesiac lady.

Christina handled the task of playing a character that asked her to mix lighter moments with heavier, more meaningful emotional beats with her signature elegance and brilliance. Her varied collection of work has grown to be recognized for its ability to subtly convey true human feeling in even the most absurd of circumstances.

Christina's most notable acting chameleon role came from her performance on the comedy "Up All Night" in the early 2010s. She delivered a master lesson in genuine, character-driven humour as the powerful CEO Reagan, navigating the challenges of juggling the demands of a demanding job with the reality of a new parenthood.

Christina Applegate has continuously broken stereotypes and confounded expectations throughout the course of her three-decade career about what a "comedic actress" can or should be. She has walked the tightrope between broad comedy and subtle drama, giving every performance an unmatched degree of dexterity, subtlety, and emotional impact.

In addition to solidifying her reputation as one of the most gifted and adaptable performers of her time, Christina has opened the door for a new wave of artists to push the envelope of what is conceivable in the entertainment business. Her adaptability is now the stuff of legends.

Impact On The Industry

In her many years in the entertainment business, Christina Applegate has become a genuine pioneer; she is a versatile actress whose impact goes far beyond the boundaries of her own accomplishment. Christina has created a lasting legacy that is still felt across the entertainment industry because of her innovative work in comedy and drama, her steadfast support of more diversity and representation, and her standing as a well-liked icon.

Christina initially came to public attention and established herself as a major comic powerhouse when she landed the role of the sassy yet endearing Kelly Bundy on the popular sitcom "Married... with Children". She might have been a one-dimensional cliche, but week after week, her physical comedic skills, perfect timing, and unexpected emotional depth gave it fresh life. In the process, Christina broke stereotypes of what a "dumb blonde" character may be and improved the character as well.

Beyond Christina's performance, her work on "Married... with Children" had a significant effect on the television business in general. A new generation of boundary-pushing, envelope-pushing comedies that questioned social norms and customs were made possible by the show's outspoken, irreverent brand of comedy. In the years that followed, a plethora of other iconic comic characters were inspired by Christina's immediately identifiable Kelly Bundy.

Christina's influence, however, went well beyond the television industry. She persisted in looking for parts that would let her go beyond the conventional notions of what made a funny actress. From the broad humour of "Mars Attacks!" to the more subversive wit of "Anchorman," Christina showed a surprising range that defied simple classification.

She paved the way for a new wave of artists who refused to fit into preconceived notions about the profession or be restricted by it by doing this. The comedy industry has become more inclusive, diverse, and boundary-pushing on both large and small screens because of Christina's courage to take chances and question the existing quo.

Christina's influence, meanwhile, goes beyond her acting career. In addition, she has consistently spoken out in favour of more empowerment and representation, especially with regard to how women are treated in the entertainment sector. Many young performers have been motivated to embrace their own distinctive features and identities by her body positive attitude and unwillingness to succumb to unattainable beauty standards.

Christina has therefore contributed to the transformation of cultural perceptions and expectations about humorous actresses. She has demolished the antiquated belief that women can either be intensely dramatic or hilarious, and that they have to pick between the two. A new generation of actors has been inspired by her to question the current quo and establish their own creative independence.

Christina has had an even greater influence on the business in the more recent years as she has continued to take on a wide variety of jobs that have shown her extraordinary versatility. Her celebrated work in television shows like "Up All Night" and "Samantha Who?" has solidified her reputation as a master of dramatic and humorous acting, encouraging a new generation of performers to aspire for the same heights.

Christina Applegate has continuously shown throughout her career that she is a real force to be reckoned with, a ground-breaking talent whose impact goes far beyond the boundaries of her own accomplishment. Her influence is seen across the entertainment business, from changing the comedy landscape to advocating for more representation and empowerment for women in the field.

Without a question, Christina's legacy will only continue to gain prominence and relevance as she pushes the limits of what is conceivable for a comedy actor. Her influence on the business is unmistakable, and she has motivated a great deal of others to pursue careers in creative and innovative fields by following in her footsteps. The effects of Christina Applegate will undoubtedly be felt for many years to come.

CHAPTER 6: MOTHERHOOD AND ADVOCACY

Balancing Career And Family

The path to fame for Christina Applegate has always been striking a careful balance between her successful acting profession and her valued personal life. From her debut as a young star on the popular sitcom "Married... with Children," Christina has struggled to balance the pressures of Hollywood with her personal life and sense of normality.

Christina initially encountered the difficulty of striking a balance between her rising stardom and the need for a secure, supportive environment when she was a cast member of "Married... with Children" in the late 1980s and early 1990s. The teenage actress had to cope with the extreme scrutiny and media attention that often accompany such success as the show's popularity soared, placing her in the bright limelight of Hollywood.

Christina, however, made the deliberate choice to maintain a solid foundation in her personal life rather than succumbing to the demands of celebrity. Nancy Priddy, her mother, who had been her pillar of support and mentor ever since she started her acting career, was still her home. Christina was able to preserve her mental stability and feeling of routine despite the craziness of her work life because of her solid home environment.

Christina never wavered in her resolve to maintain her intimate bonds with her family and loved ones, even as her notoriety increased. She was picky about the projects she worked on, making sure she had the time and resources to foster those vital relationships. As she managed the unavoidable ups and downs of life in the spotlight, Christina's approach to her job would come to be known for this meticulous balancing act.

Although Christina's acting career grew beyond the well-known role in "Married... with

Children," she remained committed to her personal life. Her relationship with musician Martyn LeNoble started in the mid-2000s, and the two were married in 2010. With the arrival of their daughter Sadie in 2011, Christina and Martyn embarked on a new chapter in their lives, complete with the trials and rewards of parenthood.

Christina was suddenly faced with balancing the demands of her successful job with the responsibilities of motherhood. Nevertheless, she faced the task with the same unwavering will that had characterised her past achievements, choosing not to let one area of her life suffer. She was picky about the projects she worked on, making sure she had time to continue pushing the limits of her profession and also be there for her family.

Christina has been open about the challenges of juggling her career and family obligations, realising that she must constantly make difficult decisions and give up certain things. However, she has also spoken about the deep feeling of purpose and pleasure that she has when she successfully blends her personal and professional life in a grounded and genuine manner.

Christina has been steadfastly dedicated to maintaining the close-knit connections that have served as the cornerstone of her life throughout it all. Whether it's spending meaningful time with her spouse and kid or keeping close relationships with her extended family, she has resisted allowing the superficialities of celebrity and prosperity to undermine her fundamental identity.

Christina has finally been able to attain a degree of longevity and job contentment that few of her contemporaries can equal because of her relentless attention to fostering her personal life. She has managed to handle the ups and downs of Hollywood with a grace and fortitude that is absolutely amazing by never losing sight of the value of family and stability.

Without a question, Christina's dedication to maintaining a careful balance between work and family will continue to be a guiding principle as she navigates the ever shifting professional environment. She has often shown that keeping a strong, enduring connection to the people and values that matter most is more important for actual success in the entertainment business than plaudits and accomplishments. Both audiences and business insiders continue to be moved by and connect with this message.

Advocacy Work

Christina Applegate has continuously utilised her position to support worthy causes and push for progress over her distinguished career in the entertainment business. Christina has become a genuine force for good, using her popularity to have a real, long-lasting influence on the world around her. Her relentless efforts to raise awareness and support for breast cancer are just a few examples of her vocal stances on body positivity and representation.

Christina's very personal battle with breast cancer has perhaps been the most important component of her advocacy efforts. The actress, who was 36 years old, was given a tragic blow when she was diagnosed with the illness in 2008, at the height of her career glory. Instead of allowing the prognosis to break her, Christina tackled the task with the same unflinching resolve that had made her name in the industry.

Christina was strongly devoted to sharing her experience and bringing attention to the significance of early identification and preventive care throughout her treatment and recovery journey. Never hiding the physical and psychological toll the experience took, she had reconstructive surgery after a double mastectomy. Christina used her experience to advocate vocally for breast cancer support services and research when she was declared cancer-free.

Christina's lobbying efforts in this field have been nothing short of astounding. Using her platform to inform and inspire others going through similar struggles, she has donated her time, money, and unfettered enthusiasm to groups like Stand Up To Cancer and the American Cancer Society. Her readiness to share her own challenges in an honest and sensitive manner has struck a deep chord with many people, motivating them to put their own health and wellbeing first.

However, Christina has done a great deal of activism outside of the breast cancer community. Using her voice to criticise unattainable beauty standards and push for more representation of many body types in the entertainment business, she has also been a resolute advocate for body positivity and inclusivity throughout her career.

Christina, a teenage actress thrown into the Hollywood limelight, saw firsthand the intense scrutiny and pressure to meet a limited, sometimes unachievable standard of physical beauty. However, she deliberately chose to take charge of her own story rather than allowing these social expectations to devour her. She used her platform to encourage and inspire women of all shapes and sizes, becoming a vocal supporter of body positivity and self-acceptance.

In this regard, Christina's advocacy work has been nothing short of revolutionary. Using her notoriety to question the established status quo, she has called attention to the detrimental practices of the entertainment business and advocated for more inclusive and representative media representations. Her openness and willingness to share details about her personal challenges and fears have struck a chord with a vast number of people, establishing her as an inspiration and source of hope.

Christina, however, goes far beyond in her advocacy activities, lending her voice to support a variety of social and political concerns. She has spoken out against racial injustice, supported significant environmental efforts, and fought for LGBTQ+ rights by using her platform. Despite everything, she has never wavered in her resolve to use her position for good and to really improve the lives of people.

Probably most impressively, Christina has made sure that her advocacy work is woven into the very fabric of her professional life, making it a mainstay of her career rather than just a side project. She's constantly found methods to make her voice heard and bring about genuine, meaningful change, whether it's via her acting roles exploring significant societal subjects or her social media presence raising awareness.

Christina Applegate's reputation as an unwavering supporter and champion of worthy causes will only continue to gain prominence and relevance as she successfully navigates the always changing Hollywood scene. Time and again, she has shown that genuine success lies not just in recognition and accomplishments but also in using one's position to improve society. She has solidified her place as a genuine entertainment industry legend by doing this, serving as an inspiration and a lighthouse for future generations.

Making A Difference

Throughout her lengthy career spanning many decades in the entertainment sector, Christina Applegate has always made use of her position to improve the lives of others around her. Christina has never hesitated to use her celebrity status to effect positive change and improve the communities she cares about, whether it be through her tireless advocacy work around important issues like breast cancer awareness or her unwavering commitment to championing causes of inclusion and representation.

Christina's very personal and passionate breast cancer campaigning has been one of the most significant ways she has left her mark. The actress was dealt a tragic blow in 2008, at the pinnacle of her career, when she learned she had cancer at the young age of 36. But Christina faced the challenge with the same unshakeable resolve that had shaped her career, refusing to let the illness stop her.

Christina never wavered in her resolve to tell her experience and spread awareness of the value of early identification and preventive care throughout her treatment and recovery. She had reconstructive surgery after a double mastectomy, never hiding the psychological and physical toll the procedure took. Christina also used her experience to become an outspoken supporter of breast cancer research and services after she was declared cancer-free.

Christina has donated her time, money, and unfettered enthusiasm to groups like Stand Up To Cancer and the American Cancer Society, and her advocacy work in this field has been very inspirational. Numerous others have found great resonance in her willingness to be transparently upfront about her own challenges, which has empowered them to place a higher priority on their own health and well-being. Christina's unwavering efforts have also contributed to the de-stigmatization of challenging discussions around breast cancer, guaranteeing that more individuals have access to the vital information and assistance they need.

However, Christina's influence goes well beyond her advocacy efforts for breast cancer. She has also consistently supported body positivity, inclusivity, and representation throughout her career, utilising her position to dismantle harmful social standards and strengthen underrepresented populations.

Christina saw firsthand the tremendous scrutiny and pressure to adhere to a limited, sometimes unachievable ideal of physical beauty as a young actress propelled into the Hollywood limelight. But she deliberately chose to take charge of her own story, refusing to allow these expectations rule her. She became a vocal supporter of body positivity and self-acceptance, using her platform to uplift and encourage women of all sizes and shapes.

Christina has done nothing less than groundbreaking advocacy work in her field. She has demanded more inclusive and representative media representations by using her famous profile to expose the damaging practices of the entertainment business. Her openness and willingness to share her personal challenges and vulnerabilities with a large number of supporters has made her an inspiration and a source of hope for individuals who have long felt marginalised and underappreciated.

However, Christina's ambition to change the world goes much beyond; the actress utilises her platform to support a variety of social and political concerns. She has strongly opposed LGBTQ+ rights, spoken out against racial injustice, and supported important environmental projects. She has never wavered in her resolve to use her position for good, always working to encourage and empower others around her.

Christina's effect is particularly noteworthy because of the way she has woven her advocacy work into the very fabric of her career. She has discovered methods to integrate activism into her artistic process, including significant social criticism and calls to action into her public image and acting roles rather than seeing it as an independent endeavour.

Christina has continuously shown a unique capacity to use her popularity for the greater good, whether it's via her acting roles to explore significant issues of identity, representation, and empowerment or her social media presence to promote awareness. And by doing this, she has solidified her position as a real icon—a performer whose influence on society will continue well beyond her remarkable body of work and define her legacy.

Christina's passion to make a difference will undoubtedly continue to expand in breadth and impact as she navigates the always changing Hollywood scene. She has repeatedly shown that real success is about utilising one's position to inspire and encourage others rather than merely collecting awards and accomplishments. Christina Applegate left behind a legacy of significant and long-lasting change in that respect.

CHAPTER 7: TRIUMPH OVER ADVERSITY

Overcoming Challenges

Over her long and distinguished career in show business, Christina Applegate has overcome several difficulties and roadblocks that would have crushed many others. Christina has repeatedly shown an unwavering tenacity and drive that have enabled her to emerge stronger than ever, despite the terrible personal fights she has faced as well as the tremendous scrutiny and expectations of early celebrity.

In 2008, at the pinnacle of her career, Christina received a sad diagnosis of breast cancer at the young age of 36. Overcoming this illness has perhaps been the biggest difficulty Christina has faced. Christina, however, decided not to allow the illness stop her from taking on the task with the same unflinching determination that had made her career.

Christina resisted letting her illness define her in the face of taxing therapies and the psychological costs of her battle. Notwithstanding the physical and psychological challenges of her ordeal, she had reconstructive surgery and a double mastectomy. Christina also used her experience as a catalyst to become a fervent supporter of breast cancer research and awareness after her cancer diagnosis.

Many followers and supporters were moved by Christina's desire to be transparent and honest about her challenges. Numerous people going through similar struggles were inspired by her unwavering attitude and her capacity to remain strong and positive in the face of such hardship. Christina made certain that her own experience would have a significant and long-lasting influence on other people's lives via her advocacy efforts.

However, Christina had several difficulties outside of her health. Since the beginning of her career, when she made her debut as the adored, stylish Kelly Bundy in the popular comedy "Married... with Children," she has been under constant strain and criticism, which might have destroyed her.

Christina faced significant scrutiny from the media and social expectations as a young actress in the bright Hollywood limelight, which might have undermined her self-esteem and confidence. It took a toll on her since she was always focused on her beauty and was subjected to unattainable body standards.

Christina chose to take charge of her own story, nevertheless, rather than give in to peer pressure. Through her platform, she challenged the damaging practices of the entertainment business and inspired women of all shapes and sizes. She became an outspoken champion for body positivity and self-acceptance.

A genuine tribute to Christina's strength of character has been her ongoing dedication to advocating for diversity and representation despite hardship. Time and again, she has shown that her determination and unwillingness to be silenced will define her, not the limited expectations of others.

Aside from navigating the ups and downs of the entertainment world, Christina has faced obstacles and disappointments in her career that would have shattered many others. She has seen a fair share of setbacks and disappointments, from unsuccessful TV pilots to underperforming box office movies.

Christina has seized the chance to develop and reinvent herself, however, rather than allowing these failures to destroy her. Fearless in taking chances and going beyond the limits of what is expected of her as an actor, she has continuously pursued fresh challenges and innovative paths. She has solidified her position as one of the most skilled and varied performers of her generation by doing this and continuing to grow and broaden her skill set.

Christina's steadfast self-belief and strong will to achieve on her own terms are the key components that have allowed her to overcome the variety of obstacles she has encountered. Her choice to forge her own path with a strong independence and tenacity that is genuinely admirable has prevented her from ever letting the expectations or opinions of others define who she is.

There is no doubt that Christina will run across fresh difficulties as she continues to negotiate Hollywood's constantly shifting terrain. She will surely come out stronger and more determined than ever before, however, if she follows her unwavering spirit. The capacity to endure hardship with elegance, fortitude, and an unshakeable sense of purpose, according to Christina Applegate, is the ultimate measure of success, not plaudits or accomplishments.

Resilience And Courage

Few artists in Hollywood's constantly changing world have ridden out the highs and lows with the unfailing bravery and perseverance of Christina Applegate. Her remarkable journey from the breathtaking peaks of her early stardom to the heartbreaking valleys of personal sorrow has shown her genuine strength of character, which has inspired many people and solidified her place in history.

The beginning of Christina's tale takes place in the late 1980s, when, as a young adolescent, she made waves in the entertainment industry as the sultry yet endearing Kelly Bundy on the popular sitcom "Married... with Children." Christina found herself struggling with the high scrutiny and pressure that sometimes accompany such rapid success after being thrust into the bright limelight of Hollywood. But despite her youth, she attacked every new obstacle with a resolute resolve that did not allow the weight of fame to overwhelm her.

Christina maintained her composure in the face of mounting pressure from the show's demands and the media's continual attention, finding solace in her close-knit family's support and her sincere love for what she did. Her career was marked by her intense independence and persistence in forging her own path, refusing to let others' expectations or views define her.

However, the years that followed would put Christina's real mettle to the test as she encountered a string of personal and professional setbacks that would have shattered many others. Christina was 36 years old when she was diagnosed with breast cancer in 2008, at the height of her career. Despite the devastating news, Christina faced the challenge head-on, bringing the same unwavering determination that had gotten her through her early years of public recognition.

Despite the difficult treatments and emotional strain of the battle, Christina never wavered in her will to win. She had reconstructive surgery and a double mastectomy, and she candidly and vulnerable detailed her story. When she eventually overcame the illness, she used her experience to become an ardent supporter of breast cancer research and awareness, utilising her position to uplift and encourage others going through similar struggles.

Christina's tenacity and resiliency were evident in every day of her advocacy work and recuperation. Rather than allowing the horror of her diagnosis to define her, she chose to use her tale as an example of the resilience of the human spirit. Countless admirers found an unwavering source of strength and inspiration in her, and her willingness to be transparently candid about her challenges struck a profound chord with them.

However, Christina had several difficulties outside of her own health issues. She has had several professional failures and challenges throughout her career, ranging from unsuccessful television pilots to movie office underperformers. Nevertheless, she has continuously seized the chance to reinvent herself and evolve rather than allowing these setbacks to destroy her.

Christina isn't scared to take chances and go beyond what is expected of her as an actor; she has often shown that she has the extraordinary capacity to change course and adapt. Whether it was her critically praised dramatic role in the television series "Samantha Who?" or her subtle comic performance in "Up All Night," she has consistently looked for new creative challenges, driven by an unquenchable desire to broaden the scope of her gifts.

Christina has an unrelenting sense of self-belief and an unflinching drive to achieve on her own terms, which are the foundations of her bravery and perseverance. Her choice to forge her own path with an incredible fierceness and sincerity is extremely remarkable. She has never let the expectations or opinions of others dictate who she is. In the process, she has not only solidified her place among the most gifted and varied performers of her time, but she has also become an inspiration and a ray of hope for young artists everywhere.

There's no denying Christina will run into more difficulties as she tries to negotiate the constantly shifting Hollywood scene. However, she will surely come out stronger and more determined than ever before, guided by her unwavering spirit. According to Christina Applegate, the real test of success is not accomplishments or honours but rather the capacity to face hardship head-on with bravery, grace, and a steadfast sense of purpose.

Inspiring Others

In the course of her three decades in show business, Christina Applegate has not only wowed audiences with her extraordinary acting abilities, but she has also been a genuine inspiration to a great number of people worldwide. Christina is a living example of the strength of the human spirit, always demonstrating optimism and empowerment via her unyielding perseverance in the face of misfortune, her unrelenting determination to utilise her platform for good, and her unabashed sincerity.

Since her debut as the glamorous and adored Kelly Bundy in the popular comedy "Married... with Children" in the late 1980s, Christina has enthralled viewers with her endless charm and extraordinary range as a performer. Her physical comedy skills and perfect comic timing had audiences in stitches week after week, and her ability to give the role real emotional nuance and sensitivity exceeded expectations.

But what really made Christina stand out was her unrelenting tenacity and elegance under duress, not to mention her obvious acting prowess. She refused to let the intense scrutiny and cultural expectations that threatened to ruin so many of her classmates define her, even as a young actor thrown into the bright limelight of Hollywood.

Throughout Christina's career, her fortitude would be put to the test several times as she dealt with a range of emotional and professional difficulties that would have crumbled even the most hardened veteran. She was 36 years old when she received the heartbreaking news that she had breast cancer in 2008, at the height of her popularity. Nevertheless, Christina faced the struggle with the same unwavering attitude that had gotten her through the difficulties of her early stardom, refusing to let the illness win her over.

Christina refused to let her sickness define her, sharing her story with unvarnished honesty and openness. She had difficult therapies, including a double mastectomy, and came out of the ordeal with a strong sense of purpose and resilience. After overcoming the illness, she committed herself to become a devoted supporter of breast cancer research and awareness, using her position to encourage and uplift innumerable others going through the same struggles.

Christina firmly established herself as a genuine inspiration to many generations of men and women throughout this difficult time. Her unshakable resilience in the face of such an overwhelming obstacle, together with her steadfast resolve to use her personal experience as a platform to change the world, struck a deep chord with her hordes of admirers who saw a mirror of themselves in her.

However, Christina's influence as a role model goes much beyond her own health struggles. She has continuously championed causes and topics that are close to her heart throughout her career, from social and political action to body positivity and inclusivity. Numerous people have been inspired by her vocal position on these issues to accept their own distinctive selves and have the guts to speak out and bring about constructive change.

Christina has always been unafraid to live out her beliefs, whether it is via her courageous support of more varied body types being represented in the entertainment business or her fervent support of LGBTQ+ rights and racial justice systems. Her unrelenting dedication to utilising her platform for good has encouraged the industry to be more sensitive to the needs and problems of underrepresented populations, in addition to inspiring her hordes of admirers.

What's most amazing, maybe, is how Christina has woven her work as an inspiration and a supporter of worthy causes into the very fabric of her career. She has developed methods to incorporate her activism and advocacy work into her acting roles and artistic endeavours, rather than seeing them as distinct endeavours. This has allowed her message of social justice and empowerment to be seen by as many people as possible.

Christina Applegate's reputation as a genuine inspiration will undoubtedly further increase as she successfully negotiates the constantly changing Hollywood scene. She has repeatedly shown that real success is about utilising one's position to inspire and encourage others rather than merely collecting awards and accomplishments. In that sense, Christina's legacy will be shaped not just by her impressive body of work but also by the significant and enduring influence she has had on a great number of people all over the globe.

Christina Applegate is a beacon of hope for anyone battling personal struggles or aspiring performers alike. She exemplifies what is possible when one has the willpower, fortitude, and steadfast dedication to use one's talents for the benefit of society. Her narrative serves as a tribute to the resilience of the human spirit and a timely reminder that everything is achievable with bravery and willpower.

CHAPTER 8: LEGACY AND IMPACT

Contributions To Entertainment

Christina Applegate has left a lasting impression on the entertainment business that is braided with tears, humour, and unflinching fortitude. Her path started as a young explosion of blonde ambition, developed into a mastery of comedy, and ended up being a monument of emotional depth.

Christina, just 15 years old, earned the part that would begin her career in 1987, playing Kelly Bundy in "Married... with Children." This ridiculous show, which was a social satire centred on a dysfunctional family, went viral. Kelly became an instant icon with her miniskirts, valley-girl slang, and bleach-blonde hair. However, Christina instilled in Kelly an unexpected tenderness and susceptibility under the surface. She was an expert at the physical humour that defined the role, including the irritated sigh, the well-timed eye roll, and the contagious laugh. Christina used "Married... with Children" as a testing ground. It demonstrated her unquestionable star power, her ability to connect with an audience, and her comic timing. The show's popularity did, however, bring with it a problem: typecasting.

Christina was itching to play parts other than comedy. She deliberately looked for tasks that tested her abilities and showed off her versatility. She experimented with romantic comedies such as "The Sweetest Thing," in which her charming comic style was a standout feature. However, she also delved into more sinister genres with thrillers such as "Don't Tell Mom the Babysitter's Dead." The publication of "Notes on a Scandal" marked a sea change. Here, Christina dropped the humorous exterior and gave a subtle performance as a cunning instructor, demonstrating her extraordinary ability to handle difficult situations. The praise she received from critics confirmed her ambition to go further into serious roles.

"Samantha Who?" served as a link between Christina's ambitions for drama and her humorous background. In her role as an amnesic lady trying to piece together her life, she tackled issues of self-discovery, grief, and identity. Her ability to skillfully combine sadness and comedy throughout the series demonstrated her range as a performer.

Christina took the crowd by surprise with "Dead to Me." She gave a real and heartfelt portrayal as Jen, a grieving widow who develops an unexpected friendship with another lady (played by Linda Cardellini). The show addressed difficult subjects including forgiveness, remorse, and sorrow. Viewers were moved by Christina's power and sensitivity, which demonstrated that she was capable of both totally redefining her image and carrying a serious main role. Her status as a gifted and versatile actress was solidified by her well praised performance.

Christina does more than just perform. She has provided the voice of animated films such as "Alvin and the Chipmunks," demonstrating her talent for giving cartoon characters a humorous personality. More significantly, however, Christina has heroically battled multiple sclerosis and breast cancer by using her position to raise awareness of these illnesses. Others going through similar struggles are inspired by her fortitude and candour.

Christina Applegate's career serves as an example of the value of going against the grain. She's a serious actor with a mean punchline, a comic who can make you weep, and a voice actress who gives cartoons life. Her journey perfectly captures the essence of an artist who is always pushing the envelope and changing. Christina Applegate continues to be a fascinating mystery, an actress who never fails to surprise and delight fans with every part she takes on, in a world that often attempts to typecast. Her legacy is one of resilience, tears, humour, and unwavering devotion to her work.

Influence On Future Generations

It is certain that Christina Applegate's impact will go much beyond her incredible career as she continues to wow audiences and make a lasting impression on the entertainment business. Through her innovative performances, her steadfast support of worthwhile causes, and her infectious personality, Christina has established herself as a pioneer whose influence will surely be felt for many years to come.

Christina first gained notoriety for her role as the adored Kelly Bundy in the popular comedy "Married... with Children." Christina enthralled audiences right away in the character of the ditzy-yet-lovable daughter by showcasing a unique combination of comic flair and emotional depth. Her physical comedic skills and exquisite timing had audiences in stitches week after week, and her ability to give the role unexpected compassion and sensitivity confounded expectations.

However, Christina's impact went much beyond her appearance on the program. She demonstrated a strength of character and perseverance that would become defining traits of her career as she managed the tremendous scrutiny and strain that came with her quick climb to prominence. Christina refused to let the limited expectations placed upon her define her; instead, she stayed true to her values of independence and authenticity, forging her own unique path and defying labels.

Throughout her career, Christina would exhibit an unrepentant attitude by taking on a wide range of parts that questioned and broadened ideas about what a "comedic actress" might be. From the broad humour of "Mars Attacks!" to the more subtle dramatic performance of "Samantha Who?," she always showed an incredible range and boldness that would go on to inspire a great number of aspiring artists.

Christina's genuine legacy, however, comes from her persistent dedication to utilise her platform for good rather than simply her acting achievements. She has often used her popularity to promote vital causes and concerns, such as more representation in the entertainment business and body acceptance, as well as breast cancer awareness and research.

The most moving illustration of Christina's lasting impact may have been her 2008 breast cancer diagnosis at the age of 36. She met the task with the same unwavering spirit that had seen her through the hardships of her early stardom, refusing to let the heartbreaking news break her. Christina, who chose to utilise her disease as a source of identity for herself and others going through similar struggles, chose to document her journey with unvarnished honesty and candour.

Numerous admirers found great inspiration in Christina's bravery and tenacity in the face of such hardship, seeing in her a mirror of their own goals and challenges. In addition to destigmatizing crucial talks about cancer, her willingness to be completely honest and sensitive about her own experience gave countless others the confidence to put their own health and wellbeing first.

However, Christina's impact goes much beyond her own health journey. She has continuously advocated for inclusion, representation, and social justice throughout her career by using her platform. She has challenged the existing quo and demanded more progressive, equitable practices in the entertainment business and beyond by using her celebrity position.

Christina has never hesitated to use her voice to bring about good change, whether it is via her vocal support of LGBTQ+ rights and racial equality or her outspoken advocacy for more diversity in media depictions. And in doing so, she has established herself as a genuine inspiration and role model for young people who want to change their communities.

Without a question, Christina Applegate's long impact will only broaden and become more significant as she continues to negotiate the always shifting Hollywood scene. She has repeatedly shown that real success is about utilising one's position to inspire and empower people rather than simply focusing on awards and accomplishments. It's about making a lasting impact on the world that goes beyond the boundaries of a single profession or job.

Christina's narrative will inspire future generations of artists, activists, and trailblazers who want to carve out their own distinctive pathways. Her unflinching fortitude, her dedication to authenticity, and her ceaseless attempts to improve the world will surely serve as an inspiration to many others, encouraging them to follow in her footsteps and strive for their own extraordinary achievements and bravery.

Christina Applegate's legacy will live on in the annals of entertainment history, not just because of her extraordinary skill as a performer but also because of the deep and enduring influence she has had on the people in her immediate vicinity. Her legacy will live on for many decades to come. She is a real icon, a source of inspiration and hope.

Remembering Christina Applegate

As a brilliant career spanning decades comes to an end, Christina Applegate's legacy will surely inspire and enchant audiences for many years to come. Christina has established herself as one of the most significant and well-liked personalities in the entertainment business with her unmatched abilities as a creative and innovative performer, her steadfast dedication to using her platform to change the world, and her unbreakable spirit in the face of hardship.

Christina's career started in the late 1980s, when, as a young adolescent, she made her breakthrough as the adored, sultry Kelly Bundy on the popular sitcom "Married... with Children." Her physical comedy skills and perfect comic timing enthralled audiences week after week, and her ability to give the role unexpected emotional depth and sensitivity exceeded expectations.

Christina refused to let the limited expectations placed on her define or categorise her, even as her celebrity soared. Instead, she stayed firmly grounded and true to herself. As she continued to push the envelope of what was conceivable for a comedy actor, taking on a wide range of parts that demonstrated her extraordinary adaptability, this strength of character would come to define her career.

Whether it was the broad slapstick of movies like "Mars Attacks!" or the more subtle dramatic work that won her praise in shows like "Samantha Who?," Christina constantly showed fearlessness and dedication to her craft, which encouraged countless other aspiring actors to pursue careers in the entertainment industry. She opened the door for a new generation of artists to declare their own distinct identities and creative ideas via her unyielding unwillingness to be limited by tradition or stereotype.

However, Christina's actual impact goes well beyond her remarkable collection of work. She has continuously advocated for worthy causes and improved the lives of people throughout her career by using her position. Her terrifying experience with the illness in 2008 served as the impetus for her unwavering support of breast cancer research and awareness, which has encouraged many others to give their health first priority and seek life-saving care.

Fans were extremely moved by Christina's bravery and openness in revealing her own cancer story because they could relate to her hardships and goals. She became a real icon, a light of hope and resiliency that echoes long beyond her last on-screen performance, because of her persistent resolve to use her experience to inspire and elevate others.

However, Christina's influence as a role model goes well beyond her contributions to the field of healthcare advocacy. Throughout her career, she has persistently advocated for inclusion, representation, and social justice by using her voice and platform, pushing the entertainment industry to be more sensitive to the needs and worries of underrepresented groups.

Christina has never hesitated to use her significant platform to bring about good change, whether it was via her vocal support of LGBTQ+ rights and racial equality or her outspoken demand for more diversity in media depictions. She has established herself as a genuine pioneer as a result of this; she is a lady whose unwavering sincerity and intense devotion to her beliefs have motivated many people to discover their own voices and use them to change the world.

As Christina Applegate's incredible career draws to an end, it is certain that her influence will live on and inspire future generations. She has made a lasting impression on the entertainment business, demonstrating that real success is about utilising one's platform to empower and elevate others rather than merely collecting awards and successes.

Christina Applegate is now considered a true icon, a living example of the human spirit's ability to triumph over the most difficult obstacles, thanks to her incredible performances, her unwavering fortitude in the face of hardship, and her ceaseless efforts to improve the world. Aspiring artists, activists, and trailblazers who want to follow in her footsteps and make their own lasting impression on the world will continue to find inspiration in her narrative.

Christina Applegate's legacy will live on in the annals of entertainment history, not just because of her extraordinary skill as a performer but also because of the deep and enduring influence she has had on the people in her immediate vicinity. She is a living legend, an inspiration to others, and a brilliant example of what can be accomplished with unflinching will, bravery, and a strong drive to change the world. She will be honoured and recognized for this for many decades to come.

CONCLUSION

The sheer scope and profundity of Christina Applegate's unique legacy astounds one as her extraordinary life and career come to an end. Christina's journey has served as a tribute to the strength of resiliency, honesty, and a strong dedication to utilising one's platform to make a real impact. It has taken her from the dizzying heights of early celebrity and success to the terrifying hurdles that threatened to derail her.

Christina's first rise to fame in the late 1980s was sparked by her breakthrough performance as the adored Kelly Bundy in the classic comedy "Married... with Children". Her physical comedy skills, perfect comic timing, and unexpected emotional sensitivity enthralled audiences week after week, breaking expectations and upending preconceived notions of what a "dumb blonde" persona might really be.

But despite her meteoric rise to popularity, Christina resisted being boxed in or limited by the particulars of that one memorable role. She continuously looked for demanding and interesting projects to work on throughout her career, which gave her the chance to fully express her abilities. From the broad humour of "Mars Attacks!" to the more subtle dramatic work that won her praise in shows like "Samantha Who?" Christina showed an incredible range of skills that encouraged a great number of aspiring actors to pursue careers in theatre.

However, what really solidified Christina's reputation as a genuine idol was her unfailing tenacity and perseverance in the face of hardship. She was 36 years old when she received the heartbreaking news that she had breast cancer in 2008, at the height of her popularity. Christina, however, faced the challenge with the same unwavering determination that had seen her through the hardships of her early stardom, refusing to let the illness overcome her.

Christina refused to let her sickness define her, sharing her story with unvarnished honesty and openness. She had difficult therapies, including a double mastectomy, and came out of the ordeal with a strong sense of purpose and resilience. After overcoming the illness, she committed herself to become a devoted supporter of breast cancer research and awareness, using her position to encourage and uplift innumerable others going through the same struggles.

Numerous admirers found great inspiration in Christina's bravery and tenacity in the face of very difficult personal obstacles, as they saw a mirror of themselves in her difficulties and goals. Her steadfast dedication to use her personal experience as a chance to effect change solidified her reputation as a genuine source of inspiration and hope, a live example of the human spirit's ability to triumph over the most difficult challenges.

However, Christina's impact goes well beyond her own health journey. She has continuously championed a broad variety of significant topics throughout her career, from social and political action to body positivity and inclusivity. Numerous people have been inspired by her vocal position on these issues to accept their own distinctive selves and have the guts to speak out and bring about constructive change.

Christina never hesitated to use her significant platform to question the status quo and call for more progressive, equitable practices, whether it was her fearless support of LGBTQ+ rights and racial justice or her ardent advocacy for more representation of diverse body types in the entertainment industry. By doing this, she has established herself as a real trailblazer—a woman whose unwavering genuineness and intense devotion to her beliefs have motivated countless numbers of activists, artists, and changemakers to pursue careers in similar fields.

It's certain that Christina Applegate's impact will inspire and echo for many years to come when her incredible career finally comes to an end. She has made a lasting impression on the entertainment business and beyond, demonstrating that real success is about utilising one's position to empower and elevate people rather than merely collecting awards and successes.

Christina Applegate is now considered a true icon, a living example of the human spirit's ability to triumph over the most difficult obstacles, thanks to her incredible performances, her unwavering fortitude in the face of hardship, and her ceaseless efforts to improve the world. Aspiring artists, activists, and trailblazers who want to follow in her footsteps and make their own lasting impression on the world will continue to find inspiration in her narrative.

Christina Applegate's legacy will live on in the annals of entertainment history, not just because of her extraordinary skill as a performer but also because of the deep and enduring influence she has had on the people in her immediate vicinity. She is a living legend, an inspiration to others, and a brilliant example of what can be accomplished with unflinching will, bravery, and a strong drive to change the world. She will be honoured and recognized for this for many decades to come.

Made in the USA
Monee, IL
13 December 2024

73578626R00059